Understanding Freud

Hervé Castanet - Yves Rouvière

Understanding Freud

ISBN: 978-2-31501-370-8
"Understanding/Graphic essay",
a collection directed by Luis de Miranda
© Max Milo Éditions, Paris, 2024
www.maxmilo.com

To Jacques-Alain Miller, whose struggle
keeps psychoanalysis alive

Introduction
Why Freud?

Sigmund Freud was born on May 6, 1856 in Freiberg, Moravia (Austrian Empire), and died in London on September 23, 1939. **His name is inseparable from his discovery of the *unconscious*, and the consequences he drew from it: *psychoanalysis*.** Psychoanalysis has always had its detractors and opponents, but today in France we're seeing massive attacks aimed at discrediting it once and for all, and associating it with the private person of its creator. For example, a *Livre noir de la psychanalyse (Black Book of Psychoanalysis)* was published in 2005, and a self-professed anarchist philosopher recently presented Freud as a dangerous pervert, manipulative and lacking in scientific rigor. At the same time, a new theory—*cognitive-behavioralism*—aims to offer a clinical alternative to psychoanalysis, by combining descriptions of neuroscience and the effects of behavioral conditioning. It legitimizes short, effective therapies applicable to everyone. These new attacks have one thing in common: their epistemic poverty, their ignorance of the ideological underpinnings at work, their belief in men and women reduced to their brains. What's new is that these attacks are echoed, vividly and sometimes laudatorily, in the media and public opinion. The aim is explicit: to do away with the great man and show—at last!—how psychoanalysis is a fraud. Indeed, psychoanalysis doesn't fit in with the ideology of the times. It doesn't please the masters who dream of a world in which the lullaby of sleep becomes a policy of *all's well—sleep, sleep little man, don't make any more noise, just sleep!*

Is psychoanalysis in trouble? Are practices being emptied of patients? Have hospitals and other dispensaries excluded it from clinical practice? Not at all. Psychoanalysis is active and alive. Some patients owe their lives to it. Others, without it, would continue to sleep and make their lives a dream. Psychoanalysis is not set in stone. She is interested in the world and the new forms of its malaise. She doesn't give up where therapeutic results are not guaranteed *a priori*: severe psychoses, autism, etc.

Herein lies the paradox: the evidence for the effectiveness of psychoanalysis is well known, but the scientistic ideology

THE MASTERS OF SUSPICION

In this book, we propose to unfold what is at stake in the Freudian discovery. Nothing could be further from psychoanalysis than the idea of objectified clinical knowledge, free from the case-by-case encounter. This book is not a summary of Freud's life or work. Its direction

is precise: how did Freud encounter the Other Scene, the unconscious? What consequences did he draw from it? We'll unfold some of these consequences for the clinic, pointing to the unheard-of that is deposited there. This unheard-of thing has a name: *psychic causality*. This expression should make us understand that, although man has a brain, he is not his brain. His specificity is to be a subject who speaks, and who is a subject only because he speaks. At one and the same time, he is subject to the language in which he dwells, and, through speech taken from language, he can be the subject of desire. "To this end, it [psychoanalysis] must remain free of all presuppositions of an anatomical, chemical or physiological nature, as something foreign to it", asserts Freud.

This reading of Freud cannot do without the teaching of Jacques Lacan (1901-1981), whose "return to Freud" enabled psychoanalysis to rediscover the radicalism of its creator, and generations of analysts to avoid wandering into clinical practice. To read Freud with Lacan is to read Freud with rigor—*to the letter*. What discoveries are we going to make about the lives of the singular "parlêtres" (Lacan) that we are?

1

The Transfer

To "understand Freud" is a seemingly simple statement —it would be a matter of understanding Freud's thought and, once understood, transmitting it as detailed, rigorous knowledge, with its advances and its stumbling blocks. It would be a matter of understanding Freud as one might understand Aristotle, Hegel or Marx. What such an assertion ignores is **the specific knowledge produced by Freud and, above all, how he himself went about inventing this new knowledge, which is called *psychoanalysis*.** The rule is not to ask this question: what's the point of finding out how an author managed to think this or that, since what counts is the regulated transmission of knowledge freed from the contingent, private conditions of its elaboration. A chemist can be unaware of Pasteur's life and still perform pasteurization operations perfectly;

similarly, consumers benefit from sterilization without knowing how it affects microbial quantities. The proper name of a scientist becomes the designation of an autonomous chemical technique. Is psychoanalysis to Freud what pasteurization is to Pasteur? The answer is both yes and absolutely no. Let's unfold this paradox.

Psychoanalysis falls within the field of rigor, which it explicitly borrows from science. It produces concepts, logical reasoning and conclusions. It seeks evidence and constructs operations to verify its hypotheses. It rejects some hypotheses and retains the most heuristic. Freud, who trained as a doctor and spent six years as a physiological researcher in E. Brücke's laboratory, never wavered from these scientific principles. In 1915, in his *Metapsychologie*, in which he attempts to lay the conceptual foundations of psychoanalysis, he writes: "We have often heard the following demand formulated: a science must be built on clear and clearly defined fundamental concepts." There's no contesting his choice: Freud defines himself as a scientist in the same way as a physicist. As a good epistemologist, he adds: "In reality, no science, not even the most exact, begins with such definitions. Nevertheless, the ultimate aim is to arrive at definitions that can then be modified. The concept of **drive** is a prime example. Freud writes: "There is one

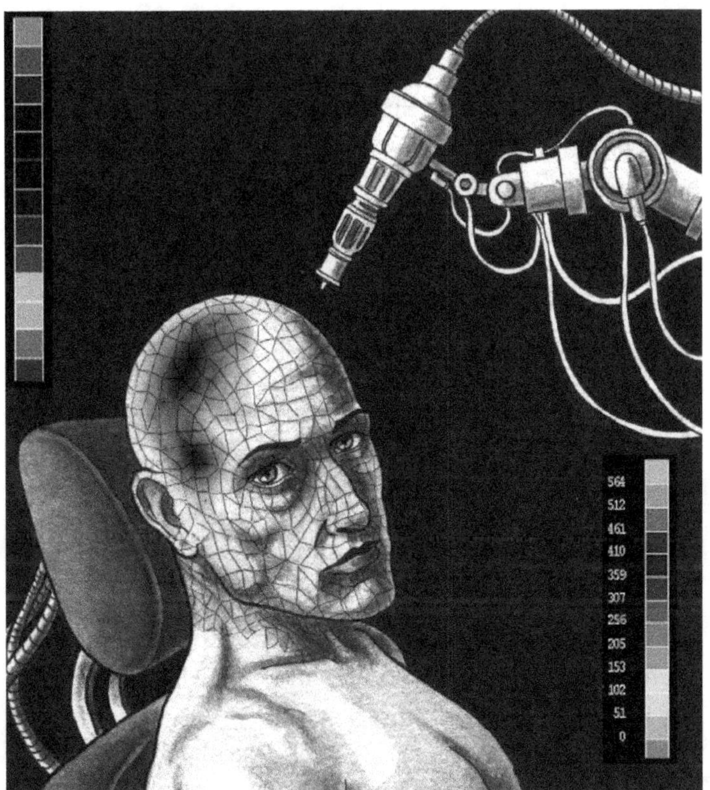

fundamental conventional concept of this kind, still rather confused for the moment, which we cannot do without in psychology: it is that of the *drive*. Let's try to give it some content, approaching it from various sides." The result is a decomposition of the drive into four terms—*impulse, goal, object, source*—the articulation of which involves an unprecedented montage between psychic life and the living body. The concept of drive thus serves as the foundation of *Metapsychology*, opening up new perspectives. The knowledge of psychoanalysis, presented in this way, "gives the pleasing impression of a serious, high-level scientific work", as Freud observed at the end of his life. It's knowledge like any other, but it differs in its object—psychic life—and not in its scientific method. As such, it can be understood, worked on and passed on.

So why did we say "absolutely not" to this understanding of Freud and his discovery? Because **the knowledge in question does not lie outside—it is not an object of the world (like a star or a molecule)—of the observer. It is the most intimate of each of us**. It cannot be learned from a book, but through experience, which is first and foremost always a test. We can read Freud as an epistemologist by seeing how his clinical work is inseparable from the scientific and philosophical context of his time. This research has its credentials, but, by definition, it ignores how Freud made his discovery, how he was intimately involved in it, in his life and in his thinking. It takes blood, flesh and suffering —in short, the living—to understand what Freud understood, and what no one before him had wanted to grasp. In 1887, Freud was thirty-one years old. Since 1886, he had

been working as a medical neurologist in Vienna, treating "neuropaths". "My therapeutic arsenal consisted of only two weapons: electrotherapy and hypnosis". He sought to build up a clientele to feed his rapidly growing family and, clinically, to learn the etiology of the observed symptoms that hypnosis was trying to suppress. **In this context, Freud met Wilhelm Fließ**, an ear, nose and throat specialist from Berlin, two years his junior. They struck up a correspondence, consisting of two hundred and eighty-seven letters and numerous scientific manuscripts, which lasted until

1904. They held regular working meetings to discuss their respective advances. Freud looked forward to them: "It's magnificent! And do you know a more beautiful place for it than Salzburg? We'll meet there and go wherever you like for a few days"; "But I'll never give up on you; […] In the meantime, write to me, make proposals and stick to this simple thing that I want to establish right away as the only one that counts: this year too we must see and talk to each other." The seventeen-year bond between Freud and his friend is of decisive importance for the birth of psychoanalysis. Freud, without realizing it (at least at first), without wanting to, fell in love with Fließ, based on the knowledge he attributed to him. The Berlin doctor develops a biological theory of female (28 days) and male (23) periodicity, which have their counterparts in the nose. There would be relationships between sex and the nose, which nasal therapy would have to verify in order to treat current neuroses! This theory about sexuality, women and mothers is delusional and paranoid. Yet it's this Fließ that Freud posits as the address for his own ongoing discoveries. **He was his private friend, his systematic reader, his acknowledged mentor—"You are the only other, the alter"**—"I hope," Freud wrote to him in his second letter, a month after their meeting, "that we will have a rich and intense relationship in the future. I still don't know how I won you over […] But I'm very happy about it. I've always had the good fortune to find my friends among the best, and I've always been particularly proud of that good fortune." Fließ's encouragement is essential to him: "It comforts me very much that you recognize the theory of constraint representations, I obviously miss you all the time during such work." In other words, Freud's scientific development does not take place in the cold—it is not a purely theoretical reflection in dialogue with reference authors. To write for Freud is to write for Fließ, to seek his reactions, his opinions, his advice, his reproaches, his disagreements. **Without Fließ, Freud's knowledge cannot be extracted from the trial-and-error research that exhausted him.** On one occasion, he told him that his findings on "nasal neurosis", founded in the biological substratum, constituted the foundation on which the column of psychoanalysis could be erected! Yes, Freud, though not inclined to be blind, would not dispute the Berlin doctor's ramblings; for him, they constituted knowledge about the sexual, which he was trying to make the psychic spring of the etiology of neuroses. Not without difficulty: "You're right, the correlation between obsessive neurosis and the sexual does not always appear so clearly. I can assure you that it wasn't easy to find [...]; anyone looking for it in a less monoidal way than I did would have missed it. Freud's "you're right" to his friend—**the sexual etiology of neuroses is Fließ's**

hypothesis, and Freud's compass. But it's not the same sexuality we're talking about: "You're the biological, I'm the psychic". We've tried to imagine that Freud's self-analysis, from which psychoanalysis was born, took place between himself and himself, without any outside intervention. Many psychoanalysts wanted to believe in this pastoral at the cost of censoring this correspondence. *The complete Letters* were only published in English in 1985, and we had to wait until 2006 to read them in French! The true Freud/Fließ story reveals that Freud's "original analysis" (the formula is O. Mannoni's) was a love transference which, by placing the Berliner as the "subject supposed to know", as J. Lacan put it, gave him the position of analyst. Fließ was Freud's psychoanalyst at a time when psychoanalysis and the cure had not yet been invented, and without his knowing it himself! **There is no such thing as self-analysis—for an analysis to be possible, the analyst's place must be clear and embodied**; this was the German medicaster— "I still hope in you as in the Messiah", Freud proclaimed to him. This transference of love, with its passionate outbursts, jealousy, disappointed expectations and overestimation of the interlocutor, enabled Freud to give shape to his thinking and clinical research. The question remains: what does Freud find? followed by: what effects does this discovery have on the Freudian subject? The picture becomes bleak.

Freud was in a bad way, his bearings no longer holding—he had somatic complaints, ideas of death, severe psychic depression: "A period of intellectual paralysis like this had never before presented itself to me. And every line is torture for me"; "I'm stupid"; "I now feel truly rootless"; "I live here, grief-stricken and in the dark"; "I still don't know what happened inside me; something from the depths of my own neurosis stood in the way of progress in the understanding of neuroses, and you were involved somehow." What these sentences testify to is unheard of. **Freud seeks to unravel the etiology of neurosis. The sexual is involved. But not only. The hypothesis of an Other scene outside the field of consciousness and reason emerges.** There are active sexual thoughts whose effects do not cease and which do not belong to consciousness. Freud discovers the unconscious in two ways: he makes this assumption for his own patients, whom he sees for ten hours a day, and he encounters this "darkness" at home. On the one hand, there are no patients, and on the other, the distanced doctor who observes. He is similar to those he treats—"I then had that feeling that patients complain so much about, that of being internally bound, and I was really distraught." **Nobody makes friends with their unconscious.** The expression *my unconscious* suggests that the subject has an unconscious at his disposal, that he is its master. As Lacan reminds us,

the unconscious is always that of the Other. Freud is patient for Fließ. He doesn't give in on what he has to decipher of the unconscious in its acted formations in transference:

symptoms, missed acts, slips of the tongue and, the royal road of access, dreams. Psychoanalysis is born of this singular deciphering process, which is always difficult and sometimes unbearable. Psychoanalysis arises from the refusal to accept the *"I don't want to know"* of the ego, from the struggle against resistance. For Freud, unravelling the mystery of dreams is not just another project. If he succeeds in doing so by analyzing his own, then he will have become the first reader of the unconscious—the one who agitates it. He will have found a cure for his own neurosis, and can be the psychoanalyst of his patients. "My self-analysis is in fact the most essential thing I have at the moment, and it promises to acquire for me a very great value if it reaches its conclusion." Hagiography would have us believe that Freud alone invented psychoanalysis, and that Fließ was an "accident" (E. Kris's terrible word). He was not. **Indeed, at the beginning of any analysis, there is transference!**

2

The Unconscious

THE DISCOVERY OF PSYCHOANALYSIS, not without a transference (Freud's first to Fließ), is that of the unconscious. It is commonplace to read that Freud did not invent the unconscious, that the term *(Unbewußte)* existed long before him and that philosophers and psychologists, mainly German-speaking, had given precise definitions of it. For the nineteenth century, Schelling, Nietzsche, Schopenhauer, Herbart, Helmholtz, Fechner, Wundt and Carus are often cited. This remark, used to discredit psychoanalysis, is perfectly accurate. The fact remains that Freud discovered the Freudian unconscious, and that this discovery makes psychoanalysis possible. No one before Freud had defined the unconscious as he did. So what is it? Freud gives it the status of a hypothesis, refusing to equate it with an unknown territory akin to the deep, dark, still waters of the isolated

ACTE MANQUÉ
LAPSUS
LAPSUS
RÊVE
RÊVE

lakes beloved of the Romantics. **On the contrary, the Freudian unconscious is action**: "The repressed representation remains, in the *Ics*, capable of action", he writes in his *Metapsychology*. **The unconscious doesn't leave us in peace; it's not wisely dozing off, taking orders.** In other words, there are "psychic representations" whose presence the subject is unaware of, but which never cease to manifest themselves. Repression accounts for this: "Psychoanalysis has taught us that the essence of the process of repression does not consist in suppressing or annihilating a representation representing the drive, but in preventing it from becoming conscious. There are representations representing the drive that consciousness stops and represses. Later, in his Second *Topica* of the 1920s, Freud called this instance of repression the *ego*. This repression is not definitive—what is repressed returns and manages to do so by disguising itself in various ways. As such, **repression and the return of the repressed are two sides of the same psychic mechanism.** The unconscious has not disappeared—its action continues. What returns has a name: the *formations of the unconscious*. What are they? Answering this question will reveal why certain representations of the drive are repressed and others are not. Why these and not these? The sexual is involved...

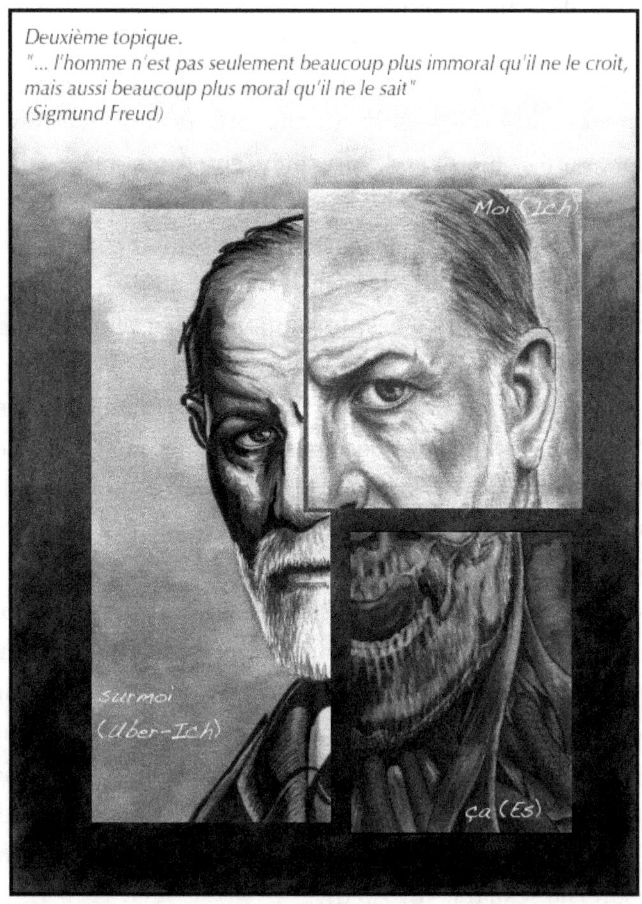
Deuxième topique.
"... l'homme n'est pas seulement beaucoup plus immoral qu'il ne le croit,
mais aussi beaucoup plus moral qu'il ne le sait"
(Sigmund Freud)
Moi (Ich)
surmoi
(Über-Ich)
ça (Es)

The dream

Freud was determined to demonstrate that the unconscious is at work in the most ordinary psychic life, and not just in neurosis. In 1900, he published his masterly study *The Interpretation of Dreams (Traumdeutung)*. It's a difficult book with an assertive theory, in which he uses his own dreams rather than those of neurotics, despite having interpreted over a thousand dreams of his patients. Dreams offer him a privileged opportunity to demonstrate that dreams are interpretable and that a general method can be derived from the hypothesis of the unconscious. This method is by no means a new dream key, which proceeds on the basis of pre-established symbols that are valid in all cases (buzzing bees = good news for the dreamer; calendar = sign of great loss of money). **A thesis unfolds: the dream's content is a *satisfaction of desire*, its motive is a *desire*.** Freud opens the *Traumdeutung* with one of his dreams, the **"injection given to Irma"**. What kind of desire satisfaction is involved? It's 1895, and Freud is treating a family friend, Irma, with psychoanalysis. The treatment ends with half-success. Irma had lost her hysterical anguish, but retained organic symptoms. On one occasion, Otto, a young doctor and friend of Freud's, gave him news of Irma, saying, "She's better, but she's not really well." It was a hard blow. Freud understood these words as a criticism of his treatment and, beyond Irma's case, of psychoanalysis. He decides to write a report justifying his clinical choices and method. With this in mind, he falls asleep and, towards morning, has a dream. The main elements of the dream to be isolated are:

—Freud meets Irma at a party. He takes her aside and reproaches her for not accepting his "solution". By refusing to listen to Freud, she suffers for it.

—Irma is bloated, pale and complains of pain in her throat, stomach and belly.

—Freud became concerned, suspecting an organic disease that he had missed. He examines the patient's throat and finds a white spot and extensive crusted formations.

—Freud calls in Dr. M., who confirms the observation. It's an infection, but future dysentery will eliminate the poison.

—The infection resulted from Otto's injection of propyl, propylene… propionic acid.

—Freud saw the chemical formula for *trimethylamine* printed before him.

—The final scenario insists that Otto's negligence is to blame for Irma's illness (the syringe wasn't clean; how light-hearted to practice like that!).

How does Freud analyze his dream? He takes it sentence by sentence, and lets his associations, made up of memories, correlations of ideas, diurnal remnants, come to him. In short, he let what his psychic life brought to him come to him—everything. **He submits to the rule of *free association*, refusing to sort, to censor, to accept only what is logical and rational.** Fourteen long pages are needed to unfold this interpretation. The dream tightens

"Every successful dream is a fulfillment of the desire to sleep." (Sigmund Freud)

around the chemical formula for trimethylamine, reduced to a series of letters printed as in a scientific book. This word-formula sums up what's troubling Freud. But how? Here are the associations: Freud talks about his friend Fließ (without giving his name) who discovered that this substance is one of the products of sexual metabolism. Trimethylamine brings out the "sexual factor and its omnipotence" always involved in the causation of neuroses. Irma is a very young widow. Otto, who reproaches her, may have set his sights on her, and would like to change her situation—to see her cured, to try his luck with her. And there's more. Freud has had Fließ observe Irma to find out whether her gastric pains are not of nasal origin! It sounds like a dream. But no! Freud continues to assume that Fließ knows something about sexuality, particularly female sexuality, as he writes of him: "[…] he has offered science the demonstration of extremely remarkable correlations between the nasal turbinates and the female sexual organs […]". Fließ, above all, was ill. He suffers from "nasal suppurations" that worry Freud; he fears for the health (risk of cancerous metastases) of his friend, his only interlocutor!

The interpretation falls: it's a dream in which Freud denies, one by one, all his possible responsibilities in Irma's semi-healing, and takes revenge for all the reproaches with justifications: 1. Irma is organically ill; psychoanalysis can do nothing about it. 2. Irma's widowhood explains her condition.

Freud can't change it. 3. Otto is responsible: he injected the wrong product with a dirty syringe. 4. Otto and Dr. M. know nothing about psychoanalysis. Freud scorns them. Only Fließ knows anything about the situation. 5. Irma's character hides another, more docile hysteric known to Freud. If Irma doesn't get better, it's because she opposes the cure.

Freud takes his revenge. The dream multiplies the means to achieve this: "Get rid of these people, replace them with three others chosen by me, after which I will be absolved of the reproaches I don't want to have deserved!"

The associations are not exhausted. Other characters and themes appear. Freud even admits that he doesn't give us all his innermost thoughts. Let's remember the demonstration: **this dream is logically interpretable**; it is the *satisfaction of a desire* (in this case, the unconscious desire to clear one's name, to take revenge on one's accusers...).

Forgetfulness, slips of the tongue, missed gestures

In 1901, Freud wrote his *Psychopathology of Everyday Life*, which went through nine editions, including additions and clarifications until 1924. In it, he continues to decipher the unconscious at work, playing with words and even letters of the alphabet—an unconscious that knows neither day nor

night, that does not rest, that insists—an unconscious that is hard-working, multiple, varied; in short, baroque. **Nothing is fortuitous; the unconscious has the last word.** In everyday life, Freud picks out what is often dismissed as unimportant, meaningless, inattentive—the little nothings of forgetfulness, errors, slips of the tongue, missed gestures and so on. They are, as J. Lacan, "stumbling, failure, crack. In a spoken or written sentence, something stumbles. Freud is magnetized by these phenomena, and that's where he looks for the unconscious. He elevated them to the status of formations that can be seen in everyone. In these formations, the logic of unconscious chains unfolds. **These little things are by no means insignificant. They betray an unconscious desire that demands to be fulfilled.** Like dreams, forgetfulness, slips of the tongue and other missed gestures can be interpreted. They're not just the prerogative of neurotics. During the years when psychoanalysis was being discovered, Freud "depathologized" the unconscious, which took on the status of a determining system for understanding psychic life, including normal life.

The Psychopathology of Everyday Life lists thousands of these little nothings. For example, **the omission of** the name *Signorelli,* which opens the book. Freud, on a trip to *Herzegovina,* is talking to a companion about Italian towns, and in particular Orvieto, whose cathedral is famous for its frescoes on the last ends. Freud wants to quote the author of the frescoes, Signorelli. But he couldn't, and two other painters' names sprang to mind: *Botticelli* and *Boltraffio.* When the forgotten name is recalled, Freud immediately recognizes it as correct. Freud could have contented himself with a banal explanation in which fatigue, inattention, memory, would have explained the forgetfulness. But he goes about it differently. He doesn't give in on the knowledge at stake, which has to be extracted from banal oblivion. **Why does the word *Signorelli* disappear into the unconscious?** Why is it repressed? Why do substitute names appear? As with the dream, Freud adheres to the rule of free association. He says what comes to him. What had he been talking about just before he forgot? The walls of the *Bosnian* Turks who, faced with sexual impotence, prefer to die. The reference to death took him back to the terrible news he had received a few weeks earlier in *Trafoi*: one of his patients had committed suicide because of an incurable sexual disorder. The associations continue, the associative chains knot and overlap—never in any particular way. Freud summarizes them in a diagram:

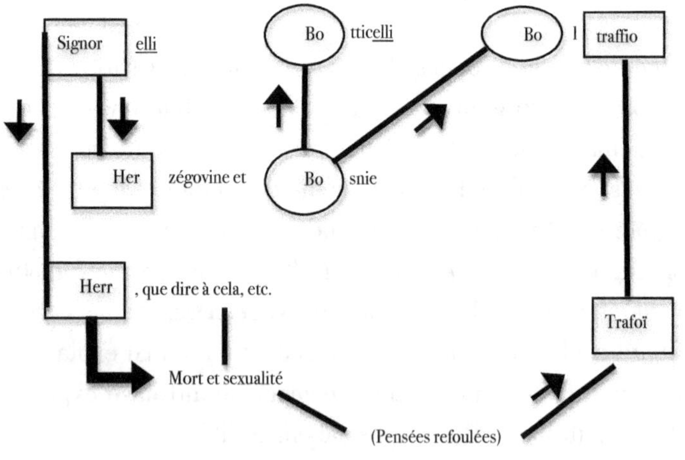

Despite his subjective vacillation, he doesn't hesitate to give the spring of the psychic process at work: **"I wanted to forget something, I had repressed something. In truth, I wanted to forget something other than the name of the master of Orvieto.** What is this something else? It's the knot between death and sexuality. *Signorelli* is forgotten against his will. On the other hand, Freud wanted to intentionally forget his *responsibility*—that his patient had died because he, Freud, had been unable or unwilling to cure him of his sexual disorder or, at the very least, to enable him to cope with it. The repressed theme, *via* the associations and assonances between words, came into play and connected with *Signorelli*—the repressed element associatively seizes the sought-after name, which is dragged into the repression.

Dream interpretation, forgetfulness, slips of the tongue and other missed gestures demonstrate the unconscious. The most particular, the most intimate, reveal general psychic mechanisms. No one can make friends with the unconscious—it will always remain Other. In 1933, Freud wrote: "We call unconscious a psychic process whose existence we must assume because [...] we deduce it from its effects, but know nothing about it."

3

Sexuality

WE OFTEN HEAR PSYCHOANALYSIS EXPLAIN PSYCHIC LIFE, in all its manifestations, from the simplest to the most complicated, in terms of sexuality. Its axiom is that "everything is sexual". Any reading of Freud is a far cry from the pansexualist cliché in which C.G. Jung, his former disciple, indulged with his immemorial sexual archetypes. **First of all, Freudian sexuality is not reduced to observable sexual practices**, to what happens when bodies meet in bed. It is never raw, isolable in a laboratory, but inseparable from a fiction, a "sexual theory"—the Freudian term for the theories that children conjure up to explain the enigmas of conception, birth and the difference between the sexes. **Next, the sexual is distinguished from the genital.** Freud has shattered the belief in a unified sexuality under the primacy of genitality aimed at reproduction, which the expression "sexual instinct" lends credence to for the animal world. The Freudian definition is much broader: "In psychoanalysis, the term *sexuality* has a much broader meaning, and differs completely from the popular meaning. [...] We consider as belonging to the domain of sexuality all manifestations of tender feelings deriving from the source of primitive sexual emotions. [...] We use the word *sexuality* in the broad sense of the German word *lieben* ('to love') [...]", Freud wrote in 1910. He added in 1920: "[...] may we remind all those who, from their lofty heights, cast a disdainful glance at psychoanalysis, how close the expanded sexuality of psychoanalysis is to the *Eros* of the divine Plato [...]". Similarly, he corrects a mistake that is too often attributed to him: if the dream is the realization of a desire, it is wrong to add that this desire always has a sexual content, or that it can be traced back exclusively to sexual impulses. In short, not everything is sexual, and sexuality is not limited to the genital.

For both men and women, because they are speaking subjects, sexuality is difficult. It's not the perfect meeting of needle and thread. **A problematic relationship with sexuality is not a possibility for men and women. It's an inescapable fact of life.** The rock of psychoanalysis' discovery lies in this point: *sexuality is never just that*. There's a problematic subjectivation of anatomical sex

for the speaking beings that we are. The idea of a natural sexuality, as observed in animals, with its rhythm, its periods, its systematicity, its repetitive instinctual fixity, is a myth—often a pastoral one in which everyone knows what to do with their sexual body and that of their partner. This myth fascinates. In a letter to E. Jones, Freud notes: "Anyone who promises to free mankind from the trials of sex will be welcomed as a hero, and will be allowed to speak— no matter what nonsense he spouts." Freudian sexuality is psychically *traumatic*, and this is the form in which it is most often encountered. By *traumatic*, we mean a lived experience that manifests an excitation so strong that no elaboration can deal with it, and thus permanently disrupts the management of psychic energy. For the principles of pleasure and homeostasis that condition psychic equilibrium, it is unassimilable. Is psychoanalysis to be credited with a radical pessimism about sex—a new way of putting the curse on it? By no means.

To address sexuality, Freud invented the concept of drive *(Trieb)* and added that of *libido*, defined as the force (or energy) through which drive manifests itself in psychic life. With these concepts, human sexuality is thought of in a way it had never been before: it is no longer one and the same, and is not born with puberty during the maturation of the male and female genitalia. The reference to normal sexuality alone (= the union of the genitals in heterosexual mating) explains nothing. The normal/abnormal criterion is irrelevant to the drive. **With Freud, sexuality**

is denaturalized. It is human, and therefore problematic, because it confronts the unassimilable. Here's proof: the "sexual aberrations" (deviations from the sexual object or goal) that make up perversions, as Freud calls them in his *Three Essays on Sexual Theory* (1905-1925), are not animal or monstrous practices. They are, in fact, fully human, and the moral language (religious, ideological, legal) that sets them apart from the norm wants us to believe in a human

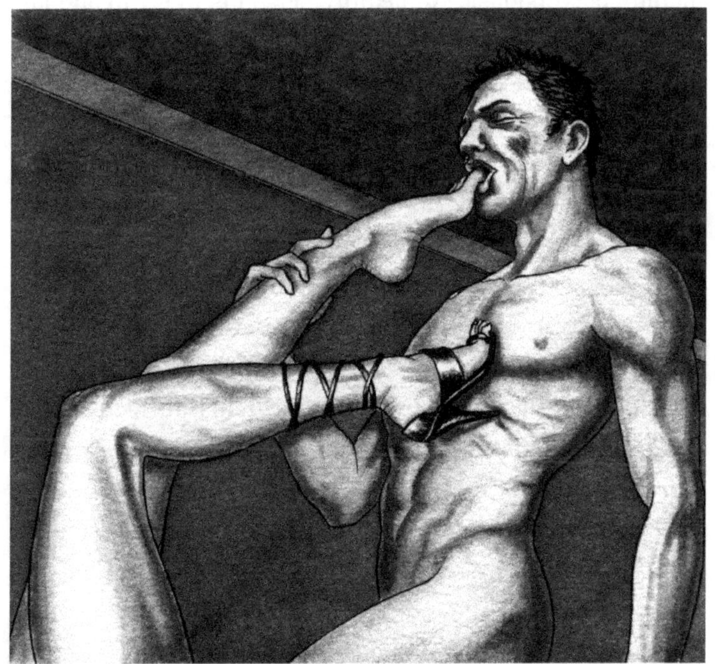

nature legitimized by a transcendence present from all eternity. Freud hammered it home (and his formulations are still radical today): "For aesthetic reasons, one would like to be able to impute this aberration to the mentally ill, as well as other serious aberrations of the sexual drive; but this is not possible. Experience shows that the sexual drive disorders observed in the latter are no different from those of healthy people, whatever their race or condition." Neuroses include perversions: "No healthy person is likely to add any kind of perverse supplement to the normal sexual aim, and this general trait is in itself sufficient to denounce the absurdity of a reproachful use of the term *perversion*." Freud is not saying that perversion and neurosis (the "healthy" ones) are equivalent. He posits that the sexual drive, as such, is not subject to the normal/abnormal criterion, and that the neurosis/perversion distinction is an effect of the struggle between the sexual drive and certain psychic resistances— "It is permissible to suppose that these forces participate in relegating the drive to within the limits deemed normal [...]". **The constant reference to perversions in the *Three Essays* is crucial in defining human sexuality.** Without them, so-called normal sexuality is incomprehensible, unless we dream of it as subject to procreation—"It turns out, without forcing the issue, that normal sexuality emerges from something that existed before it [...]". Perversions, by dissociating object and goal and recomposing them in a multitude of ways (inversions, paedophilia, anatomical transgressions, fetishes, fixations on preliminary sexual goals, etc.), isolate the components of all human sexuality. There's a "connection", says Freud, between perversions and normal sexuality!

How do the concepts of drive and libido dismantle sexuality as a goal aimed at reproduction? **Why, for psychoanalysis, is there no sexual synthesis—no total drive?** The sexual drive is not an unbreakable block, nor is it archaic or primordial. It is a montage, a bricolage, an assembly of various heterogeneous components—just as much a circuit, an apparatus. J. Lacan likened it to a "surrealist collage" with no head or tail. Imagine a dynamo connected to a gas socket, activating a peacock feather that tickles a woman's belly. Under the pressure of movement, the mechanism transforms: the lady's mouth becomes a gas socket, and a rump emerges in the middle. It's a beautiful comparison that takes the impulse out of an Epinal imagery where everything is smooth, habitual and pre-formatted. In fact, Freud isolates the components of the drive: 1. the *thrust*, which is the driving factor—a "piece of activity". 2. The *goal*, which is always satisfaction to appease the excitation. 3. The *object*, which is that in which or by which the drive aims. "It is what is most variable in the drive, and is not originally linked to it [...]"

4. The *source* understood as the somatic process localized in an organ. Each of these elements can undergo transformations, have a specific destiny. Nothing is pre-established as to the use of the thrust; it is a raw state ready for psychic processing. The means of achieving the goal (= satisfaction) are multiple; they can be derived, suspended, combined, exchanged, active or passive. **If the object is not originally linked to the drive, then the latter is radically different from instinct, which links goal and object.** It can change, be replaced, at any moment in the drive's destiny. It can be a foreign object or a part of the body itself. As for the source, it can cling to any part (inner or outer) of the living body, regardless of the genitalia.

There is no such thing as monolithic sexuality. Only the impulses thus cobbled together can inscribe the sexual in the unconscious: "[…] they are numerous, stemming from multiple organic sources, they first manifest themselves independently of one another and only later are brought together in a more or less complete synthesis. The goal that each of them pursues is the attainment of *organ pleasure*." **These descriptions explain how the Freudian drive is *partial***—always partial in relation to biological purpose; how satisfaction is *unfocused* and coupled to an autonomous erogenous zone—any organ can play this role.

Is this partial definitive? Freud's answer is yes.
Is it not possible to find a synthesis, a totalization of the
scattered components of the drive? No. *Metapsychology*
will distinguish between the field of drives and that of
love, which effectively creates a unity, a way of assembling
the disparate. Love, on the other hand, is not impulsive.
It belongs to the ego and is narcissistic. While it may be
"intimately linked to the activity of subsequent sexual
impulses", it belongs to that field where it's a question of
loving oneself through the other, where there is reciprocity
between *loving* and *being loved*. The drive field, on the other
hand, is pure activity—the ego is excluded. Sexuality is
therefore partial and perverse. Love makes us dream of a
synthesis that's finally possible… but it's not sexual! Freud
maintains the heterogeneity of the two fields.

**A clinical consequence: "The child has his sexual
impulses and activities from the very beginning, he
brings them into the world with him and it is from
them that proceeds [...] what we call the normal
sexuality of the adult."** This is why Freud defines the
child as a *polymorphous pervert*. This expression has been
overused. It was taken to mean that the child was a preco-
cious depraved person, a pervert (in the sense of the perverse
practices of adults), and morality took offense. Such a thesis
could not be accepted as general. However, it simply draws

the consequences from the partial, polymorphous nature of the drive; infantile innocence is lost. This did not stop criticism. Innocence had to be restored. Infantile sexuality was Freud's invention—his forcing.

The proof? Adults don't remember. Forgetting is the proof. Infantile amnesia about sexuality is related to the unconscious and to the ego's repressive authority. It is even rich in lessons, as it opens the way to understanding what is repressed in neurosis—**"Without infantile amnesia,**

there would be no hysterical amnesia", admits Freud. Among the manifestations of infantile sexuality, Freud distinguishes, for example, *sucking* (and auto-eroticism), of which he makes a "model". Voluptuous sucking appears in infancy and can continue into adulthood. It consists in the rhythmic repetition with the mouth of a sucking action that has no alimentary purpose. Sucking is not the result of unquenched hunger. This activity involves the lip, tongue or any other reachable part of the body—including the big toe. Often, it's joined by clutching, with simultaneous rhythmic tugging of another person's lobe or body part. This sexually satisfying sucking leads to sleep and even to a kind of orgasm, since sensitive parts of the body, including the genitals, can be rubbed. Sucking then opens the door to masturbation. **By focusing on one's own body parts, sucking is *auto-erotic*.** How did it come about? It's fuelled by the search for a pleasure already experienced—that of suckling on the mother's breast, in which the *erogenous zone* was the child's lips. This satisfaction of sucking is based on this previous satisfaction of the need for food, from which it then frees itself. What's more, after suckling, the child manifests a sexual satisfaction that serves as a prototype for all other satisfactions. Freud goes so far as to write: "Sucking at the mother's breast becomes the starting point of the whole sexual life, the model never reached for all subsequent

sexual satisfaction [...]". The advantage of choosing body parts is to free the child from the outside world, which it has little control over. What are the consequences for future life?

If the fixation with this satisfaction remains, the adult will enjoy kissing, drinking or smoking. If repression intervenes, then disgust for food will turn into hysterical vomiting. This brief example demonstrates three characteristics of infantile sexual life: it is built on the *support of* a vital bodily function; it has no externally constituted sexual object, and is therefore *auto-erotic*; its sexual goal is limited to a single *erogenous zone* outside the genital primacy.

Perversions and infantile sexual life enabled Freud, *through* the dismantling of the drive, to establish that the unconscious writes nothing about being male or female. **The unconscious does not write the difference between the sexes. The drive is definitely partial!**

4

Hysteria

THE ENCOUNTER BETWEEN HYSTERIA AND CLINICAL DISCOURSE DOESN'T DATE BACK TO PSYCHOANALYSIS—it can already be found in old Hippocrates! In Freud's time, not a single psychiatric textbook made any reference to it, often in irritated terms: the hysteric, generally a woman (the Greek word for uterus *is hysterion*—hence *hysteria*), was described as dissimulative, caught up in demands, opposition, staging, theatricalization of the body (the famous reflex arc), provocative intrigue and so on. The doctor's word is devalued, contested, falsified. The doctor, in the position of master, distrusts it, and the battle of truth (that of the concept, of the curative aim) against falsity (the patient's lie) begins. Freud, during his stay in Paris in Charcot's department, had witnessed these battles from which the master wanted to emerge victorious. Popular parlance has taken up this description, likening the hysteric to a pain in the ass.

REVE
été 1881
SOUVENIRS
ecole 82
Hiver 1889
1876
vacances

Without hysteria, psychoanalysis would not have been possible. These women's words, so often considered worthless, had to be listened to, posited in their dimension of truth, for a new clinic to emerge. This choice marked a break with previous medical practices. Freud insists on the need to go into the smallest details to grasp the determination of hysterical symptoms. It's not a question of listening to patients and then silencing them in the name of knowledge that has already been established. They're the ones who have to say everything that comes to mind in associative mode. They are the ones who know, even if they consciously ignore this unconscious knowledge. Truth oozes from every detail. It has to be discovered and deciphered, and that means constantly asking for new details. There's a transition from a clinic of the gaze, where semiological observation takes precedence, to a clinic of listening, where the word is truth.

A precise description of Freud's approach to hysterics, and the implications for the development of the psychoanalytic technique, can be found in his *Études sur l'hystérie* (written in collaboration with Joseph Breuer), published in 1895. **In them, we discover an active, lively and determined Freud, a veritable detective seeking to uncover unconscious blind spots and other mysteries of repression.** He never gave in, questioning, insisting,

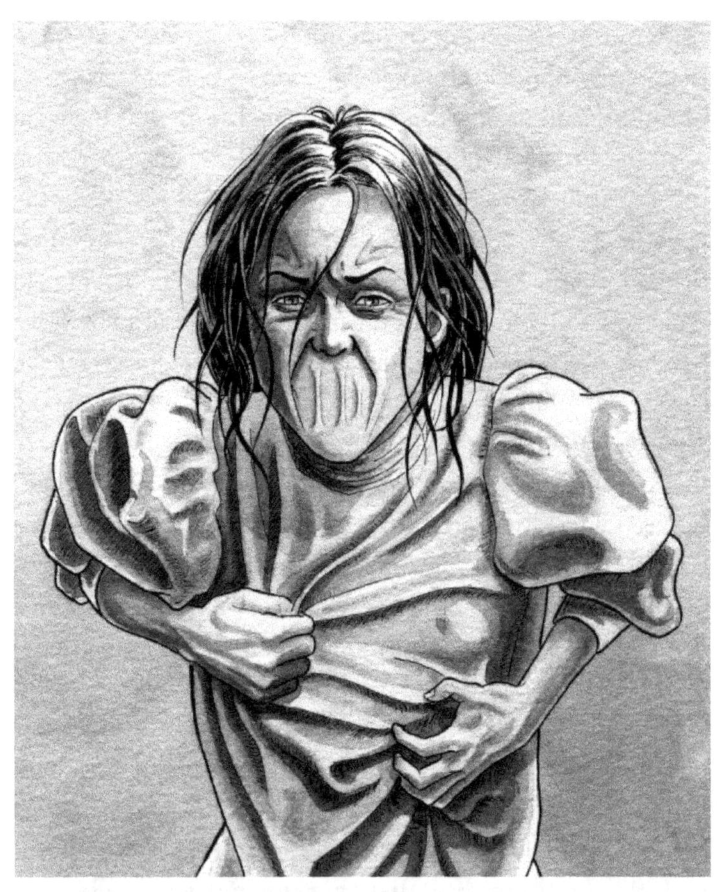

demanding words (not confessions) from the young women who approached him. He refuses nothing they say— memories, complaints, reproaches, descriptions of organic suffering, dreams, futile associations and so on. Freud uses cathartic hypnosis to overcome the resistance to forgetting childhood memories, which is the (traumatic) cause of the hysterical phenomenon. Hypnosis makes them reappear in their original freshness, making them accessible to treatment—"[…] each of the hysterical symptoms disappeared immediately and without return when we succeeded in bringing to light the memory of the triggering incident, in awakening the affect linked to it and when, afterwards, the patient described what had happened to him in great detail, giving verbal expression to his emotion". This is why, as Freud and Breuer put it, "the hysteric suffers above all from reminiscences"—reminiscence of the non-verbalized (non-abreacted) trauma.

This encounter with hysteria wasn't all plain sailing, and Freud himself was roughed up, criticized and let down by these young women who didn't take kindly to the diktats of self-confident knowledge. In fact, it was one of them who forced Freud to abandon hypnosis in 1889, limiting his sessions to free association. Forty-year-old Emmy von N. writes to herself in an anguished voice: "Don't move! Don't say a word! Don't touch me!" She was telling Freud that it was up to her to say what she wanted, and that he was there to collect her words. The analytical technique was born, and it was to the twenty-four-year-old Elisabeth von R. that he would apply it: "I was therefore able to give up hypnosis immediately. [...] First, I had the patient tell me everything she knew, carefully noting passages where an association remained enigmatic, where a link seemed to be missing in the chain of motivations; then I pushed further into the deeper layers of memory. [...] The story of suffering told by Fräulein Elisabeth was very long, and interwoven with all kinds of painful events. During her accounts, she was not in a state of hypnosis [...]". The principle of the analytic session has been invented.

The question remains: what is the specificity of the reminiscences from which the hysteric suffers? Breuer did not answer this question; for him, the internal cause of hysteria remained unknown. Freud alone provided the answer: the sexual is involved. **In other words, the cause of hysteria is sexual. In all cases? Yes!**

It was in 1905 that Freud published his master book on hysteria, which verified this thesis. Constructed like a play with all its twists and turns, **the "Dora" case remains a theoretical and clinical compass for analysts, thanks to the breadth of its demonstrations**. Today, it's fashionable to consider that clinical research, on the model of the hard medical sciences, is built on the most recent discove-

ries made around the world. A good scientific article, for example in immunology on the mechanisms of the AIDS virus, needs to be in dialogue with the international work, written in standard English, of the last three or four years. What value, then, can psychoanalytic clinics have when they tirelessly return to Freud's texts, which are more than a hundred years old? How can we approach and treat hysteria today if analysts' compass is still fixed on a text written in

German in 1905? Aren't psychoanalysts confusing living, ongoing research with a rather dead (epistemological) history of ideas and concepts? These remarks apply to immunology, genetics and neuroanatomy, but not to psychoanalysis. However, psychoanalysis does not make Freud into an unsurpassable bible in which everything has been said and demonstrated. **Psychoanalysis is first and foremost Freudian and, as far as unconscious psychic mechanisms are concerned, the passage of time may have modified the concrete forms in which they manifest themselves, but it has not transformed the causes that produce them.** On the contrary, some research explicitly seeks to annul Freud's discovery, either by discrediting its inventor (Freud as a sex patient, projecting his private rantings onto the psychic life of humanity), or by substituting other explanatory systems (cognitive and behavioural theories, for example). These (often obscene) deconstructions find echoes in our societies, including among clinicians. Hence the need to return, once again, to Freud, in order to answer the question: why are these criticisms of psychoanalysis finding their authors and an audience today? Because, firstly, thinking is becoming impoverished, less demanding and confusing the scientism of these new explanations with the accomplished forms of science; because, secondly, psychoanalysis doesn't appeal (and never has) to the masters who want to dream (and make us dream) of a padded world where everything is possible—if not immediately, at least in the near future. **The Freudian discovery—** that the paradigm of the relationship between the One and the Other, the sexual relationship, cannot be established; that sexuality is not that; that the symptom is both the proof and the attempt to continue believing in it—**introduces a radical bone into all the pastorals of happiness, of *everything being simple, of aiming for the possible within reach.*** The reality of psychoanalysis is the basis of a politics of freedom, even as it demonstrates that the unconscious never ceases to stir, to act, to condition those actions that the subject believes it can master and keep on a leash!

Pro domo plea, the critic will say. Let's return to young Dora and the unheard-of things she discovers in her brief analysis, interrupted by her patient. No master can make this patient go softly. **How does Freud conduct this treatment?** Dora (real name Ida Bauer—1882-1945) was the daughter of a textile industrialist. Her brother Otto, a year and a half older, would become a leader of the Social Democratic movement and Foreign Minister. By the age of eight, Dora had already developed "nervous disorders" with permanent respiratory suffocation. She would later multiply the symptoms (known as conversion symptoms) that affected her body: dyspnea, nervous coughing, aphonia, migraines and so on. She took over her brother's usual infectious diseases. He would start these illnesses, and she would finish them. Freud first saw her in 1898 (she was sixteen) for a persistent cough with hoarseness. He suggested psychic treatment, but abandoned the idea, as the attack disappeared spontaneously. He saw her again when she was eighteen in 1900. Dora had become a beautiful, intelligent girl with independent judgments, who didn't hesitate to mock the doctors' inability to cure her. **She's depressed, has**

character disorders (dissatisfied with herself and her family), is tired, lacks concentration and cuts herself off from contact with others. One day, her parents find a letter threatening suicide. They became frightened, and her father took her to see Freud. What does the analysis reveal? For many years, Dora's father has had a mistress, Mrs. K., who looks after him during his illness (venereal, contracted before his marriage). His wife means nothing to him. Mr. K., Mrs. K.'s husband, takes an interest in Dora, and on a lakeside stroll makes a declaration of love in which he, too, declares that his wife is nothing to him. Dora takes this badly, immediately slaps him and demands that her parents leave without any explanation. A few days later, she informs her family and asks her father to stop seeing Mr. K. and especially Mrs. K.—which he refuses to do. Mr. K. denies the facts and criticizes Dora as a sex maniac who has invented the whole scene. Dora's father endorses this explanation. Freud sees this incident (M. K.'s amorous advances and affront) as the psychic trauma that is the precondition for the formation of her hysterical state. But more is needed to account for her hysteria. It's necessary to draw on childhood influences that have had a similar effect to trauma. This concept of symptom causation is a departure from the Freudian explanation in which imagery tends to confine it: a traumatic event would mechanically produce the formation of a symptom. **The demonstration is more devious: it takes a series of elements, the articulation of which is to be specified in each case, to produce a symptom.** At least two are needed: the second triggers a mechanism that recovers and revives repressed psychic traces. **For Freud, there is no unambiguous causality, but rather a causal *overdetermination*.** And what about Dora? A few years earlier, when she was only fourteen, Mr. K. managed to be alone with her, taking advantage of the opportunity to hold her close and kiss her on the mouth. Dora felt intense disgust and ran away. She told no one about this first scene—except Freud during a session. Symptoms appear following this kiss: 1. She eats reluctantly, has a slight aversion to food. 2. She feels pressure on the upper part of her body. 3. Finally, she avoids passing by a man in tender conversation with a lady. How does Freud interpret these three symptoms? The *disgust* comes from the repression of the erogenous zone of the lips (this zone having already been mobilized by infantile sucking). The *pressure* is linked to the sensation of Mr. K's virile organ on his body, which must have aroused Dora's clitoris during the kiss. It has been moved to the chest. *Phobic avoidance* reflects the fear of coming face to face with a man in a state of sexual arousal. It helps avoid confrontation with the repressed perception.

Freud multiplies his questions, and Dora responds, often in a matter-of-fact way, reporting two dreams that masterfully expose her subjective position. Freud's analysis revolved around the very detailed interpretation of these two formations of the unconscious. Dora begins by reproaching her father, wanting to ignore Mr. K.'s attitude towards her in order to maintain her relationship with Mrs. K. Her complaint is that she is practically a prostitute to Mr. K. so that her father can continue his sexual affair. **Lacan's 1951 reading of the case takes this initial reproach as the starting point for unfolding the young patient's unconscious logic, as revealed in Freud's *dialectical conduct of the treatment*.** This takes the form of three *developments of truth*, leading to *dialectical reversals*: 1. Freud rejects the hypocritical lie of the father, who had presented Mrs. K. to him as a mere friend. He takes Dora seriously in opposition to the family lies, and addresses her (first dialectical reversal): "Look at your own part in the mess you're complaining about!" 2. The patient blames herself because she had become complicit in the relationship, babysat the K.'s two children, didn't go to their house when her father was there, and so on. Dora doesn't want to open her eyes. The Dipian relationship shows her identified with her father. So why this jealousy? Second dialectical reversal: this jealousy conceals a love interest in someone other than the father. 3. Her fascinated attachment is to Mrs. K., whose confidante she is and who provides her with knowledge of sexual matters. The dialectical reversal produces this discovery: Dora attributes to Mrs. K. the "mystery of her own femininity". Dora's question is: what does a woman want? What does it mean to be the object of a man's desire? Mrs. K. embodies these questions. Freud misses this essential point when he repeatedly deflects his patient's desire onto Mr. K. He wants to believe in a victory of love. Ah! if Mr. K. had insisted on Dora, he hopes, she would have finally given in to him and acknowledged her own love. **Unwilling to see Dora's homosexual link to Mrs. K., Freud doesn't allow this third dialectical reversal to open up a new development of truth. So Freud was wrong? Yes, but it's from Freud that we draw this conclusion from his "technical error", as he puts it; it's his conceptualization that allows us to read his error and substitute another way out. Freud teaches us to read Freud!**

5

Obsessional Neurosis

As early as 1894-1896, Freud firmly established the etiology of neuroses: "Their symptoms arose through the psychic mechanism of (unconscious) *defense*, that is, through the attempt to repress an irreconcilable representation which had come into painful opposition with the patient's ego." This representation is sexual in nature. In hysteria—as in Dora's disgust—there is an "experience of sexual passivity". It is "troumatism" (Lacan). **In obsessional neurosis, on the other hand, there is pleasure-taking, experienced participation in sexual acts. It's *"sexual activity"*— it's *"tropmatism"* (Lacan).**

Dr. Ernst Lanzer, a twenty-nine-year-old law student, was Freud's patient known by the emblematic name of **"the rat man"**. The story of this treatment, published in 1909, is woven into the opposition between the two people this patient

cherishes most: his father (who had died a few years earlier) and his lover Gisela Adler—whom Freud calls his "lady", probably in reference to the lady of courtly love for whom the knight writes his most beautiful poems and performs his greatest feats of conquest. Lanzer has been passionately in love with his lady for many years. He devotes a "respectful love" to her—in other words, he loves her, but never touches her. He keeps the use of the organ to himself. In concrete terms, "he has intercourse infrequently and at irregular intervals. Prostitutes disgust him. In general, his sex life has been poor; onanism, at sixteen or seventeen, has played only an insignificant role. His potency would be normal; the first coitus took place at twenty-six". It was not to be an easy cure. The patient insulted Freud and his family, and sent him death wishes, but the work continued.

Lanzer suffers from a severe, rather incapacitating obsessive neurosis. **Freud is the true inventor of this neurosis, in which regressive thoughts replace acts.** These thoughts themselves are continually sexualized. *Only sexuality is obsessive*: this is the axiom that obsessional neurosis verifies at every turn of the thought process. Freud publishes this case, unfolded in its entirety, to explain "the means by which obsessive neurosis expresses its most secret thoughts [...]"—those of the unconscious. With this lengthy

text, one of his five major psychoanalyses, Freud sets out to complete and continue his earlier exposés on the subject, published in 1896 under the title *Nouvelles observations sur les psychonévroses de défense (New observations on defensive psychoneuroses)*. Neurosis consists of:

—apprehensions: "He fears that something will happen to two people who are very dear to him: his father and [...] [Gisela specifically]",

—obsessive urges, such as cutting one's throat with a razor",

—prohibitions on trivial matters".

This lady obsesses him. She occupies his thoughts. He broods over her. He obsesses about her all the time, and the years go by: this merry-go-round has been going on for ten years now.

What was our patient's infantile sexuality? In his second session, Lanzer reports a conflict from his earliest memories, when he was six or seven years old. It involves women and his father, "the person he cherished most in the world". This father, whom he says "would have given up all happiness in life if it had saved [his] life [...]". Little Ernst is inquisitive; he glances steadily at the maids who look after him, he goes under their skirts to wear out his eyes on their *pudenda*; he has "an ardent and torturing curiosity to see the female body": "I still remember the extreme impatience I felt, at bath time, waiting for the governess, undressed, to enter the water [...]". Freud notes: "We see this child in the grip of a component of the sexual instinct, voyeurism, whose manifestation, appearing repeatedly and with great intensity, is the desire to see naked women who please him." **How can we explain the obsession that would later arise, in other words, how can we explain this destiny as an obsessive neurotic?** Freud's answer is clear: this desire does not exist alone. It is accompanied by that which opposes it, that which opposes it, that which prohibits it. "However, opposition to this desire is already forming somewhere, since a painful affect regularly accompanies its appearance. It's obvious that there's a conflict in the soul of this little sensualist; for, alongside the obsessive desire, there's an obsessive fear, intimately linked to this desire: every time he thinks about it, he's obsessed by the apprehension that something terrible will happen." To sexually desire a woman—in this case, to see naked women—is to immediately make a terrible misfortune possible. **Obsessive desire and obsessive fear are inseparable.** Desire is all the more obsessive because fear is, and vice versa. Desire and fear feed off each other: hence the torturing intensity of mental obsessions. What does Lanzer fear? What would this terrible misfortune be? Freud deciphers his obsession: "If I have the desire to see a

naked woman, my father will have to die", and adds: "The distressing affect clearly takes on the character of a disturbing strangeness, and gives rise, even at this moment, to impulses to do something to avert the disaster, impulses similar to the defensive measures that will emerge later on". At this point, neurosis is actualized: "We thus have an erotic impulse and a movement of revolt against it; a desire (not yet obsessive) and an apprehension opposed to it (already obsessive in character); a painful affect and a tendency to acts of defense. It's the complete inventory of a neurosis."

Lanzer's entire emotional life, and his relationship with his female partner, will revolve around this opposition between his ardently beloved forbidding father and his choices in love. It's the unconscious wish for **the father's death** that the obsessive broods over—the mainspring of his compulsions. Thus, in the first reported example, "at the age of twelve, he loved a little girl [...], but she wasn't as tender with him as he would have liked. The idea then occurred to him that she would be more affectionate to him if some misfortune were to befall him; and the thought occurred to him that his father's death might be that misfortune". The result is not long in coming: the patient vigorously rejects this idea, which is terrifying for him to utter. Similarly, in the second example, "six months before his father's death, a similar thought had flashed through his mind. At the time, he was already in love with the lady in question, but could not contemplate a union for pecuniary reasons. The thought that had occurred to him was this: through my father's death, I might become rich enough to marry her. The answer: "He went so far as to wish that his father would leave no inheritance, so that this loss, so terrible for him, would be compensated by nothing." Third example: an idea came to him "on the eve of his father's death: I'm about to lose what is dearest to me in the world". To this, a thought opposed: "No, there is another person whose loss would be even more painful to me." It's his lady.

Freud, hearing these formulations, sweeps aside Lanzer's hesitations: **the father's death is not a fear, but a wish of the son.** For this subject, there is the coexistence of love, which he consciously proclaims loud and clear, and hatred, repressed, unconscious—"[...] it is precisely this love, so intense, which is the condition for the repression of hatred." **How can we explain this unconscious hatred?** The answer provides Freud with the unconscious logic of obsessional neurosis. First, the metapsychological observation: "It must be admitted that this hatred was linked to a cause that made it indestructible. So, on the one hand, hatred of the father is protected from destruction and, on the

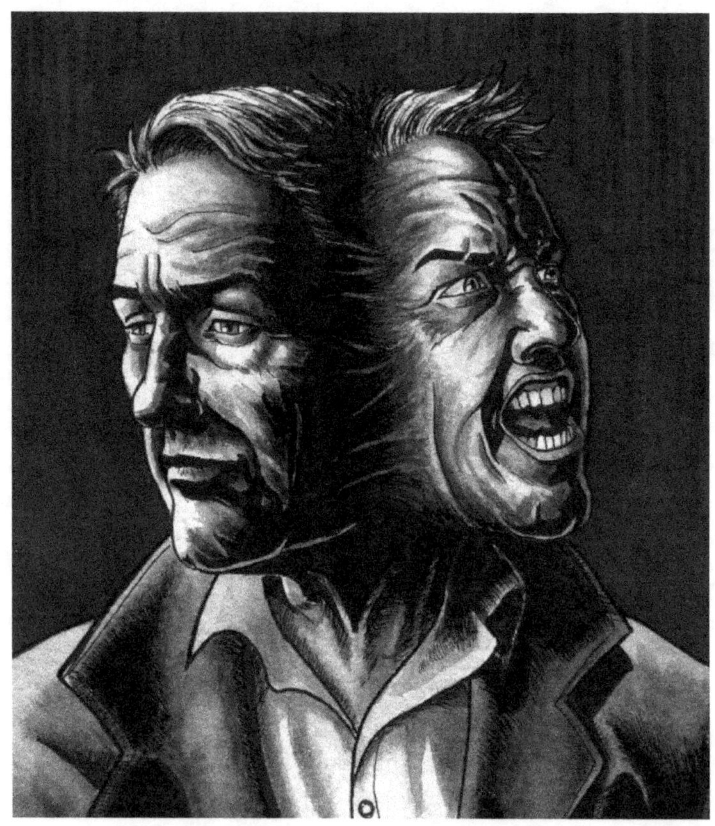

other, great love for the same father prevents it from becoming conscious. The only thing left for this hatred to do is to exist in the unconscious, from which it can nevertheless resurface, at times, like a flash of lightning." Then, the structural reason: "The source that fed her hatred and made it unalterable was obviously sensual desires; in the gratification of these, her father had seemed a hindrance. Such a conflict between sensuality and filial love is absolutely typical." Hence the ever-present infantile wish to "do away with the troublesome father".

For Lanzer, this conjunction of love and hate with his mortal wishes extends to all his love objects. So, first and foremost, to the lady of his thoughts. He confesses: "He then tells me that he remembers other impulses of revenge, towards the lady for whom he nevertheless has a love full of veneration, and whose character he depicts in an enthusiastic manner."

These cues help us to grasp the famous **"stone scene"**: "On the day of the lady's departure, our patient stepped on a stone in the street. He had to remove it from the road, thinking that, in a few hours' time, his friend's car, passing by, might have an accident because of this stone. A few moments later he realized that this was absurd, and had to go back and put the stone back in the middle of the road." This scene is paradigmatic, as it shows that "in this lover, a struggle is raging between love and hate for the same person; and this struggle is expressed in a plastic way by a compulsional act with highly significant symbolism: he removes the stone from his friend's path, but then cancels this gesture of love, putting it back in its place, so that the car runs into it and his friend gets hurt. We would be wrong to consider that the second part of this compulsion was inspired by the patient's critical sense. [...] This gesture, being compulsively performed, betrays that it was also part of the pathological action, but that it was determined by a motive contrary to that which provoked the first part of the compulsive action". The true significance of these compulsions "lies in the fact that they express the conflict of two contradictory tendencies of almost equal intensity, which are [...] always the opposition between love and hate". **This interplay of love and hate explains Ernst's relationship with Gisela**—the mainspring of their life for the past ten years: "The lady had rejected the first marriage proposal our patient had made to her ten years earlier. Since then, periods alternated when he thought he loved her intensely, with others when, even consciously, she was indifferent to him. Whenever, in the course of treatment, he had to take a step that might bring him closer to the goal of his desires, his resistance first manifested itself in the feeling that he didn't really love her, a feeling that quickly faded away."

Freud explains the case in a striking phrase: "His morbid conflict was, in fact, essentially a struggle between the persistence of his father's will and his own feelings of love." His father had indeed been his son's best friend. Everything drew them together except for one thing: Ernst's sensual desires. "It's undeniable that, in the realm of sensuality, father and son were separated by something, and that the father would have been an obstacle to the son's early development. An idea that came to the son during his first sexual gratification in coitus attests to this: **"But this is magnificent," thought Lanzer, "to experience this, one would be capable of murdering one's father!** It is in this conflict, this opposition between the supposed will of the father and the choice of a sexual object, that lies the explanation for the obsessive symptoms that paralyze the subject's life and invade his thoughts by sexualizing them. "His love—or rather, his hate—is truly all-powerful: it is precisely these feelings that produce the obsessions whose origin he does not understand, and against which he defends himself unsuccessfully." And Freud concludes: "It is in the repression of his infantile hatred of his father that we see the process that led to the neurosis of all the subsequent conflicts in his life"—including, first and foremost, his relationship with his female partner: the revered, untouched lady. **Dead father and idealized lady are inseparable**—"their two images sustaining each other, in a characteristic equivalence [...], one from the phantasmatic aggression that perpetuates her, the other from the mortifying cult that transforms her into an idol", wrote Lacan in 1953.

"La religion serait la névrose obsessionnelle universelle de l'humanité; comme celle de l'enfant, elle serait issue du complexe d'Oedipe, de la relation au père" (Freud)

The obsessional's partner-symptom is the father, whose presence is always restored by both conscious love and unconscious hatred. The obsessional spends his time, it seems, wanting to kill this forbidding father, a hindrance to the son's sexual desires. What the obsessive forgets is that the named father, the **symbolic father,** doesn't have to be killed, since he's already dead, and it's as the missing one that he can operate. He is the father who has become Other. This wish for the father's death is reduced to a simulacrum of his murder—a pantomime. By never ceasing to want to kill the father, who is already dead, the obsessional devotes himself, on the contrary, to trying to save him—to wanting him to be indestructible. The obsessional's father is not, strictly speaking, the dead father, but **the father who never stops dying, and on whom he lashes out** again and again—the father as mortified Other. Whether he loves him and/or hates him makes no difference. Love and hate are just two sides of the same coin—the only one at his disposal, the only one he uses in his exchanges, including and especially in love.

The cure restored Lanzer's taste for life and freed him from the most painful forms of his neurosis. He died in 1914 during the Great War, a prisoner in a Russian camp... He had married Gisela in 1910 after twelve years of intense courtship.

6

Perversion

We've already said it: the drive, because partial, is perverse, and the little man is a polymorphous pervert. But what about adult perverts—perverts per se? For Freud, the attitudes, behaviors, rituals and other acts that manifest the most surprising forms of human sexuality do not lead to a diagnosis of perversion. In other words, perversion is a subjective position and cannot be deduced from a series of observable practices. **Freud repeatedly demonstrated that only the subjective position—precisely the *fiction of unconscious fantasy*—could serve as a clinical compass.** In the years 1925-1927, he isolated a mechanism in which the subject says no to the discovery of maternal castration and the difference between the sexes. This is *denial* (= *Verleugnung*). Faced with the sexual difference that encounters the real, the pervert is divided. **One psychic current recognizes**

(maternal) castration, another refuses it. This yes and no (to castration) coexist in the unconscious and account for the paradox of perverse positions, notably fetishist desire.

In 1908, Freud described the effect of a boy's disco-very of the female genitalia: "I am convinced [...] that no child [...] can fail to be preoccupied with sexual problems in the years before puberty." How do they deal with them, and what answers do they come up with? Children develop "sexual theories" in which a first "surge of knowledge" can be identified: "The first of these theories is linked to the fact that the differences between the sexes are neglected [...]. [...] This theory consists in attributing a penis to all human beings, including female beings [...] The penis, already for the child, is the guiding erogenous zone, the primordial auto-erotic sexual object, and the value he attaches to it finds its logical reflection in his inability to imagine himself as a person [...] without this essential element." **What does the encounter with the female object produce?** "When the little boy sees the genitals of a little sister, his words show that his prejudice is already strong enough to do violence to perception; instead of noting the lack of the member, he regularly says by way of consolation and conci-liation: it's that the... is still small; but when she's bigger, it'll grow nicely. The representation of the woman with the penis reappears again, later, in adult dreams." **The child says no to castration**—this no is inscribed in the uncons-cious and returns in dreams (among other manifestations of the unconscious) in adulthood. The woman with the penis is a sign of this no to the (visual) perception of the difference between the sexes and the absence of a female penis. This discovery about the phantasm of the woman (mother) with a penis explains the fetishist position.

Freud cites several male patients "[…] whose objectal choice was dominated by a fetish". The patients never complained about this **fetish**. The fetish did not have the status of a symptom: "It is not to be expected that these people sought analysis because of the fetish; the fetish is indeed recognized by its followers as an anomaly, but it is rare for it to be experienced as a painful symptom." Patients consulted for reasons other than the use of a fetish. It was only in the course of analytic work that it was discovered, and then only marginally. Fetishists don't complain about their fetish for one simple reason: "Most of its followers are very happy with it, or even congratulate themselves on the facilities it brings to their love life." **The fetish poses no problem**, even if the subject admits that its use is anomalous in relation to current sexual norms. It doesn't cause complications because it has been chosen to avoid difficulties in love or sex.

What is the meaning and purpose of the fetish? The answer is valid in every case: "I'm bound to disappoint people by saying that the fetish is a penis substitute. But I hasten to add that it's not just any penis substitute, but a very special penis that has great significance in early childhood and then disappears. In other words, it should normally have been abandoned, but the fetish is there precisely to protect it from disappearing. I'd say more clearly that the fetish is the substitute for the woman's phallus (the mother's), which the little child has believed in and which, we know why, he doesn't want to give up". **The fetish inscribes the maintenance and abandonment of the belief that the woman has the phallus.** If the negation of female castration had been completely achieved, there would be no need to erect a fetish. The unconscious would inscribe this affirmation: the woman has a phallus. Clinically, this would be psychosis, and such a belief could make its way back into the reality of a hallucination. This is by no means the case in perversion: the belief is also abandoned. The establishment of the fetish, constructed by displacement, writes: the mother has the phallus/the mother doesn't have the phallus. **The fetish is a return of the repressed**, and it is in relation to repression that it must be understood: "[...] this interest is even more extraordinarily heightened because the horror of castration has erected a monument for itself by creating this substitute. The stupor before the real genitalia of the woman, which is not lacking in any fetishist, remains an *indelebile stigma* of the repression that has taken place." **The fetish is not a**

monument to the phallic mother, it's a monument to the horror of castration—proof, then, that this castration has been unconsciously affirmed. "We can now see what the fetish accomplishes and how it is maintained. It remains the sign of a triumph over the threat of castration and a protection against this threat; it also spares the fetishist from becoming homosexual by lending woman that character by which she becomes bearable as a sexual object." The fetish is a protection against the castration of which he, the subject, could become the victim. By denying female castration, it produces the phantasm of the phallic mother, from which the fetish is detached.

Freud puts it succinctly: "The study of fetishism is to be strongly recommended to all those who still doubt the existence of the castration complex [...]". The **denial of castration** is the conceptual tool for grasping the subject's relationship to his object in his unconscious fantasy as the support of perverse desire.

Here's an **early example** from Freud: "The most remarkable case was that of a young man who had erected a certain 'shiny nose' as a condition of fetish. The surprising explanation for this was the fact that, having been brought up in an English nursery, this patient had later come to Germany, where he had almost completely forgotten his mother tongue. The fetish that originated in early child-

hood was not to be understood in German, but in English; the 'shine on the nose' was in fact a 'look on the nose'; so the nose was this fetish to which, incidentally, he could at will bestow this shine that others could not perceive." The example is all the more remarkable for being based on a translinguistic pun. The German word for *shine is Glanz*; the English word for *glance* is *Blick*. This young man, who spent his early years immersed in the English language, has unwittingly chosen as his fetish a *gloss (Glanz)* on his nose, which is none other than the *glance (glance)* inaugurally cast on the radically intolerable feminine (maternal) castration. The nose is established as an *ersatz* (symbol) of the absent maternal penis. The nose, in this case, will have been what was inscribed on the ultimate image that preceded the emergence of maternal castration, and on which the gaze moved and then became durably fixed —the anatomy of the nasal organ, its prominence, offering a privileged material support for its election for this purpose. **This shiny nose both covers and reveals what it hides: the aphallic female sex.** *Glanz auf der Nase* is a screen-memory that returns, by displacement, from the repressed *glance at the nose.* In his analysis of the patient, based on his associations, Freud discovers his constitution through this passage from English to German: the shift (metonymic, following the contiguous elements of the signifying chain) is made, by homophony, from two words which, when written, differ by only two letters: *Glanz/glance.*

This *shine*, erected as a fetish, is attributed by the subject: he's not already caught up in a clinic of the visible and the obvious—as Freud says: this "shine, others couldn't perceive it". The gain for the subject, in his love and sexual life, is considerable. For him, it's a secret, kept safe from others, which, when the time comes, makes things much easier: it's a condition (in the sense of a cause) for his sexual practice. Thanks to his invisible (except to himself) fetish, he saves himself a great deal of effort—the kind of effort that overwhelms and even exhausts neurotics bound by their symptoms. As Freud notes: "The fetish [...] is easily accessible, the sexual satisfaction attached to it is easy to obtain." By blocking an image taken from the primitive scene, this fetish constitutes a monument to the maternal castration towards which this child was looking a little too closely. **With his fetish, this subject plugs the gap in the maternal Other. It constitutes an *all-encompassing* mother**, imagined as a *phallic mother*. This brilliance—inseparable from a play of reflections: light and shadow—dazzles more than it enlightens. At the moment when the horror of castration emerges, when unbearable reality manifests itself, the panic-stricken subject turns away, blinded, and fixes his gaze on the… nose: representation has been denied. The fetish has become a sign object, simultaneously affirming and negating maternal castration. In this vignette, this man has identified with the mother's phallus, and it is as phallus that he offers himself to complete the feminine Other. **Through his fetish, women have become sexually possible to him.**

Here's a **second example**: it's the case of a man "[…] whose fetish was a pubic girdle that he could also wear as swimming trunks. This piece of clothing completely concealed the genitals, thus the difference between the genitals. According to the analysis documents, this meant either that the woman was castrated or that she was not, and it also made it possible to assume the man's castration, since all these possibilities could perfectly well be concealed behind the girdle, the outline of which was the fig leaf of a statue seen in childhood. Naturally, such a fetish, doubly tied to opposites, is particularly strong. The same analysis applies as for the previous case. But this case, in addition to questioning transvestism, presents a different identification of the subject: he is not identified with the phallus (of the mother), but with the mother herself, who is supposed to possess a phallus hidden under her clothes (= under the girdle).

Finally, the pervert can identify with the imaginary father, who is thought to have castrated the mother and siblings. Freud sees an exemplification of this in the attitude of the Asian mat cutter: "His act reconciles two incompatible assertions: the woman has kept her penis and the father has castrated the woman."

These three possible identifications of the pervert derive from the phallic mother fantasy as a consequence of the denial of castration. In all cases, the feminization that results from this face-to-face encounter with the mother, and the innumerable games of double mirrors that develop, can be identified.

But perversion, according to Freud, is not an oasis of pleasure where sexuality is self-evident and trauma is excluded. A cure for neurosis does not produce a nice pervert. Quite the contrary, in fact. In 1938, in his last article (left unfinished), he insists on the unconscious price the pervert pays for playing this game of denial. He is not even with castration, which will continue to be active: "[…] in all this to-ing and fro-ing between denial and recognition, it was still castration which had found a more distinct expression […]". Compared to the neurotic, the pervert (fetishist) succeeds thanks to his fetish, but is always subject to the possible curtain-raiser, i.e. the uncon-

"Ce qui caractérise toutes les perversions, c'est qu'elles méconnaissent le but essentiel de la sexualité, c'est à dire la procréation" (Freud)

trollable emergence of the encounter with feminine castration. The fetish and its sophisticated apparatus collapse like a house of cards—the veil is torn. The real, in manifesting itself, provokes horror, triggering, as it did in the construction of the fetish, the dislodging from oneself. This is what the pervert cannot overcome—and what neurotics do: the return of the tremor that signals what, for him, remains the unassimilable feminine castration. No human subject can avoid the encounter: it's always possible, even for the pervert who's been trained to cancel it out. The pervert's panic is absolute, unlike that of the neurotic (symptom and fantasy acting as a buffer). The subject's denial is matched by the psychic trauma of the encounter, actualizing his failure. **The pervert wants you to believe he's succeeding. He demonstrates his fiasco. As Lacan put it, perversion is a crock!**

A final question arises. Why is perversion generally the preserve of men? Men are the weaker sex when it comes to the perverse structure. The reason is structural. It has to do with the girl's position in the castration complex: "It's different for the little girl. From the outset, she has judged and decided. She has seen it, knows she doesn't have it and wants to have it. [...] She notices the large, clearly visible penis of a brother or playmate, immediately recognizes it as the superior replica of her own small, hidden organ, and from then on is a victim of penis envy *(Penisneid)*." This structural position leads her more towards neurosis and the demand addressed to a man—in which the symbolic equation: penis = child will be found. **Men, as Freud teaches us, still have a long way to go in the perverse ways of desire.**

7

Psychosis

It's still common to hear that psychoanalysis is not advisable in cases of psychosis. Some clinicians (whether psychiatrists, doctors or psychologists) are willing to admit that psychoanalysis is not ineffective in neuroses, but they refuse to take the step of calling on it in proven (and a fortiori serious) cases of psychosis. Madness must remain the sole prerogative of doctors, and if a psychoanalyst has medical training, it's precisely with psychotics that he must once again become the psychiatrist who prescribes medication and ensures hospitalization. Why this purely medical prerogative? The answer is common sense: psychosis has, in their view, an organic causality. They don't refuse to allow patients to talk. At best, it can be used to support the patient in coping with whatever is ravaging him or her. Psychoanalysis is then a therapeutic complement, a psychic support within the framework of the psychiatric practice or hospital. As much as the hysteria/psychoanalysis binomial seems self-evident, the one that links psychosis and psychoanalysis appears problematic. In turn, recent forms of psychiatry only serve to render this binomial meaningless. With the DSM (Diagnostic and Statistical Manual of Mental Disorders), an international classification of mental illnesses, they are attempting to do away with specific, case-by-case theorizing, in favor of a universality of mental disorders valid across the globe and for all populations. The DSM is based on an inductive method applied to syndromic consensus. The substitution of syndromes (= the study of disorders) for nosologies (= the study of diseases) marks the disappearance of the clinical approach in favor of health as a norm, reduced to a series of items (= "statistical identification of regularities in the occurrence of pathological signs, with as great a degree of precision as possible as to the syndromes thus differentiated", as an Inserm report puts it).

Contrary to these assertions, which substitute the moralistic and statistical term *"health"* for the clinical, psychoanalysis posits another hypothesis: **there is a *psychic causality*, including for psychosis.** This causality does not exclude psychiatric medication, which provides a certain degree of comfort, or the sometimes indis-

pensable hospitalization of psychotics. **Psychoanalysis is not opposed to hospitals and confinement; rather,** it rethinks what goes on there. In 1967, Lacan was able to assert that psychoanalysis was the future of psychiatry. The psychoanalyst has a place in the hospital. Freud himself had a precise theory of madness, systematized in his famous 1911 article, "Psychoanalytical remarks on a case of paranoia (*dementia paranoides*) described in autobiographical form". This article, one of his five major psychoanalyses, is devoted to a voluminous book written by an eminent appeal court magistrate, President Schreber, who became psychiatry's most famous case. **Daniel Paul Schreber** (1842-1911) wrote his book in 1903; it wasn't until September 1910, during a trip to Sicily with his disciple Ferenczi, that Freud wanted to comment on it to derive a theory of paranoia.

What does Freud discover in this reading?

Foreclosure

For Freud, three unconscious psychic mechanisms define the three clinical structures of neurosis, perversion and psychosis. The first is repression, the second is denial, and the third is *forclusion*. **This last term translates the Freudian word *Verwerfung*, which describes the psychic causality of psychosis.** We owe this translation to J. Lacan, who, in 1955-1956, commented on Freud's article and Schreber's book in his Séminaire. In another article (dated 1918), dedicated to the "Wolf Man", Freud describes the following facts: at the age of five, this little boy, sitting on a bench next to his maid, has a hallucination. He saw his little finger cut in two, but felt no pain. He felt great anguish. Eventually, without moving, he calms down and discovers that his finger is perfectly unharmed. Freud comments on this experience by saying that the child did not repress the unbearable castration (= presentified by this cut) because "he didn't want to know anything about it in the sense of repression". Indeed, repression is symbolization. The content of the representation disappears from consciousness, but remains in the unconscious as indestructible. The unconscious chain preserves this repressed content, which sooner or later will return, like a prisoner who has disappeared from the court and is still locked away in the dungeons of the castle. What the "Man with Wolves" experiences as a child is of a different nature: **the representation is not repressed; it is therefore not symbolized, and it returns to the real.** It's not a projection; there's a rejection, an entrenchment of the psychic representation—a **foreclosure of castration. Freud adds: "Strictly speaking, no judgment was made here as to its existence [= castration], but it was as if it didn't exist." Hallucination is an elementary phenomenon of psychosis. It arises at the point where nothing in the unconscious responds to allow symbolization. (Psychotic) hallucination does not arise from an organic disorder that distorts the functioning of**

the perceptual apparatus, but from an essentially psychic mechanism.

What is foreclosed in Schreber? Reading Freud, Lacan answers that the foreclosure concerns a specific signifier—the one that holds the psychic organization together. **This is the Nom-du-Père insofar as it is the signifier that inscribes the law in language.** "What do I mean when I speak of *Verwerfung*? It's about the rejection of a primordial signifier into the outer darkness, a signifier that will then be missing at this level. This is the fundamental mechanism I assume lies at the root of paranoia. It's a primordial process of exclusion from a primordial interior, which is not the interior of the body, but that of a first body of signifiers".

Just as Schreber is about to receive a rare promotion, and the signifier of this appointment appears, **his surrounding world no longer holds together.** It deconstructs itself. One day, staying with his wife in a room at his mother's house, he hears strange noises inside the walls. He tries to find a rational explanation. All his hypotheses fall on deaf ears. What remains is this: a noise in the walls remains unexplained. It's an auditory hallucination that proves this deconstruction. This is only the beginning. Schreber's experience of subjective annihilation gets worse and worse. What has not been symbolized (i.e., having the use of the signifier of the Nom-du-Père presentified by this new title of president of the court of appeal) returns to the real, demolishing what made him stand as a man, a husband, a magistrate, a doctor of law, and so on. Foreclosure thus makes it possible to specify the clinical structure of psychosis. **With this primary compass, the psychoanalyst is no longer helpless in the face of psychosis**—he doesn't shrink back. On the contrary, by discovering what conditions psychosis, he or she has the reference points for concrete clinical work with psychotic subjects. Psychosis and psychoanalysis are no longer mutually exclusive.

Delirium as an attempt at healing

Schreber's subjective world, triggered by this prestigious appointment, has been shattered. Is Schreber powerless? Does he consent to this annihilation? Will he settle for this enigma that leaves him lost? The answer is no. Schreber elaborates a systematized, rigorous delirium—precisely the kind that his book, nearly four hundred pages long, records. **His delusion is therefore an answer.** This thesis may come as a surprise, as the delusion is worrying and signals a serious and unpromising clinical advance. There are therapies that aim to eradicate delirium, and a number of drugs do just that. Delirium is not eradicated, only contained. Such an orientation forgets the purpose of delusions for Schreber (as for any psychotic subject). For psychoanalysis, it's not a question of aggravating the delusion—of indulging in it, or even deluding oneself with the patient. It's about identifying its place and function: **"Delirium is an attempt at healing"**, says Freud. Through their delusions, psychotics attempt, in solitude, to reorder their world, to face up to the annihilation that is falling upon them. **Schreber's delusion develops a bodily transformation to which he will consent: becoming *God's wife at the request of God himself.*** Schreber's God is a special God. It's not the God of love and mercy; it's a God who, for his own enjoyment, demands this transformation of Schreber's body. "Since then, I have consciously inscribed the cult of femininity on my standards, and from now on I'll stick to it as far as the respect due to those around me will allow, and whatever people may think who don't understand considerations of the supernatural order. I'd be curious to be shown someone who, faced with the alternative of either going mad and retaining his masculine habitus, or becoming a sane woman, would not opt for the second solution." Becoming a woman with the retraction of his virile organs inside his body will enable him to be God's wife and give birth to a new race of men. As a woman, he will experience a state of enjoyment, voluptuousness and bliss that no living being has ever known:

"[…] God demands a constant state of enjoyment, as being in harmony with the conditions of existence imposed on souls by the order of the universe."

Schreber's experience is that, by touching his body, he feels it to be made up of feminine nerves geared to voluptuous pleasure—proof that his transformation has taken place: "When I exert light pressure on any part of my body, I feel under the cutaneous surface a texture made of filaments or cords [...]. By exerting pressure on this texture, I can obtain a sensation of voluptuousness on the order of that of a woman, especially if I think at the same time of something feminine." These descriptions are the richest parts of Schreiberian delirium. Freud would explain this proximity between beatitude and voluptuousness by the signifying interplay that brings the two words together in German: "This surprising sexualization of celestial beatitude gives us the impression that in Schreber the concept of beatitude might have arisen from the condensation of two main meanings of the German word: defunct and happy through the senses." Lacan has often been criticized for playing with words and deciphering in them the mechanisms of the unconscious, defined as a language. Freud's annotation about *defunt* et *heureux* makes it clear that, while Lacan reads Freud with the tools

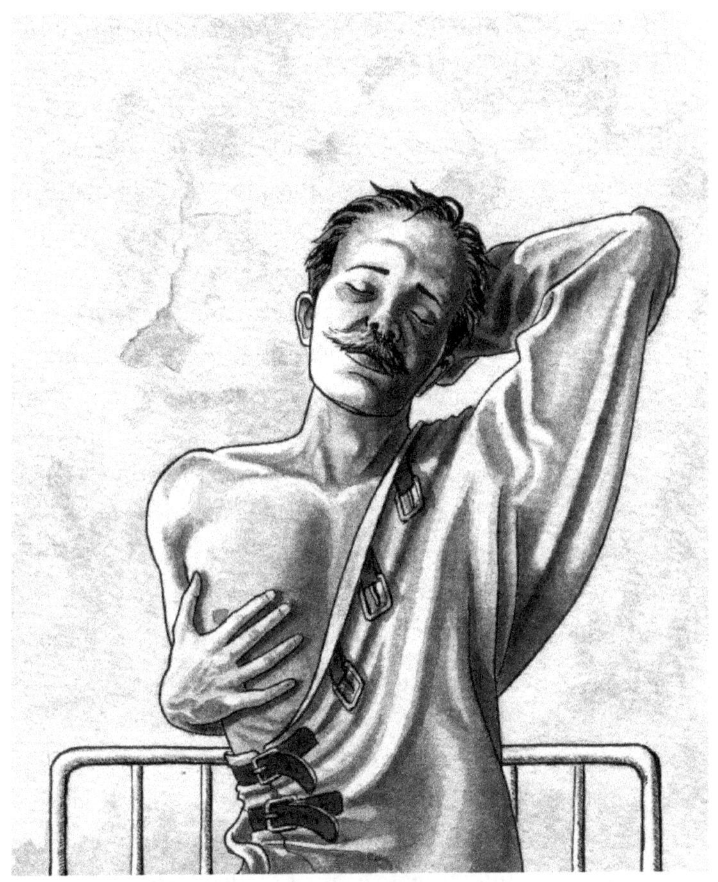

of Saussurean linguistics, he only reads what Freud has explicitly discovered!

In this delirium, there's a *"push-to-femme"*, as Lacan puts it: "At times of approach, my breasts can convince anyone of the presence of relatively well-developed breasts. "At moments of approach, my breasts can convince anyone of the presence of relatively well-developed breasts", he adds, offering himself up to the scrutiny of scientific expertise: "I am ready at any time to submit my body to any medical examination whatsoever, so that it can be verified whether my allegations are correct, according to which my entire body is traversed from head to toe by the nerves of voluptuousness, as can only be encountered when dealing with the body of an adult woman [...]". Becoming a woman in her delirium, with its power of certainty, has an immediate effect: "It's the only way for me to reach a bearable bodily condition during the day, and to find at night—at least to some extent—the restorative sleep my nerves need; *intense voluptuousness*—this is no doubt also well known to medicine—*does indeed lead to sleep.* By sticking to this course of action, I'm serving the best interests of the rays, and therefore of God himself." Schreber's acceptance of becoming a woman did not come without conflict and struggle against the God who performed miracles on his body, causing unbearable pain. There is a struggle, and Schreber opts for this choice: "[...] *in search of a reasonable compromise,* all that remained was for me to come to terms with this idea of being transformed into a woman."

Thanks to Freud, psychoanalysis has something to say about psychoses. It has to unfold the solutions that privilege the inventions and solutions, however modest and provisional, of psychotics in order to achieve appeasement, stabilization, or even a replacement for this foreclosure of the Name-of-the-Father, which, in Schreber's case, returns to the real in the terrible form of this God who wants and demands endlessly. **Psychoanalysis is perhaps at its most inventive and determined in the clinic of psychoses, including its hardest forms, such as autism.**

8

The War

What are we to make of these unheard-of results discovered by Freud on the clinical knowledge of psychoanalysis, which our seven previous chapters have unfolded? Of course, they are primarily intended for cures and the treatments that follow from them. But is that all? No. In Freud's work, there's an approach to what makes **civilization unhappy**, and not just private unhappiness. To conclude, we'll isolate what he says about the war—the war that saw his sisters die in concentration camps and forced him to flee Austria for England. **In 1932, Freud dialogues with physicist Albert Einstein on *Why war?*** Why have millions died since the dawn of time, when the horror of death rivals the atrocities committed in and for the sake of destruction? Can we finally put an end to war? And if so, how do we get rid of it? Freud's answer is to put **violence at**

A Albert Einstein

the heart of the social bond: "Conflicts of interest arising between men are therefore, in principle, resolved by violence. This is the case throughout the animal kingdom, from which man cannot exclude himself. [...] Originally, in a restricted horde, it was the superiority of muscular strength that decided what should belong to one, or whose will should be applied." Violence is not secondary, it is not one solution among others, it is the primary response—the one that cannot be eliminated. The instruments, weapons and knowledge of warfare will historically only be secondary means of amplifying this violence. Law itself, which is the social response to this blind violence, stems from it: the transition to law results from "the fact that we can compete with a stronger person by uniting several weaker ones. "Union is strength. Violence is broken by union, and the strength of these elements together represents right, as opposed to the violence of one. We see, then, that law is the strength of a community. For Freud, law does not exclude violence—it is violence in action: "[...] it is no longer the violence of the individual that triumphs, but that of the community. These remarks explain why **Freud does not believe in a socio-political organization that could eliminate the possibility of violence, and thus of war, of which it is a social form.** On the subject of Russian Bolshevism, he notes: "It seems, then, that the attempt to replace material power with the power of ideas is, for the time being, doomed to failure. It is a miscalculation to overlook the fact that law was originally brute force, and that it cannot yet dispense with the aid of force.

Freud builds on Einstein's assertion that human beings have an active principle of destruction, of imposing death. He takes up his famous theses on **Eros** and **Thanatos**. "We admit that man's impulses fall exclusively into two categories: on the one hand, those that wish to preserve and unite; we call them erotic [...] on the other, those that wish to destroy and kill; we encompass them under the terms of *aggressive drive* or *destructive drive*." **Freud distances himself from any belief in a brighter tomorrow**, when he asserts that Eros and Thanatos cannot be separated: "Now, it seems that it hardly ever happens that an impulse of one of the two categories can assert itself in isolation; it is always 'linked', to use our expression, to a certain quantity of the other category, which modifies its goal, or, as the case may be, alone allows it to be accomplished." The conclusion is radical: "[...] it would be pointless to pretend to suppress man's destructive tendencies. Should we put up with them, never limit them? Is the Freudian thesis cynical enough to admit the worst, even to the point of turning away and letting it realize its power to kill? Would psychoanalytic discovery

be, at this point, in the active service of death? This is by no means the Freudian position. Affirming Thanatos does not mean submitting to it or amplifying it. How does Freud respond to Einstein? "From time immemorial, mankind has undergone the phenomenon of the development of culture. [...] It is to this phenomenon that we owe the best of what we are made of and much of what we suffer." Yes, **Freud's answer to death is culture (the German term *Kultur* is sometimes translated as *civilization*).** The thesis is asserted with undiminished determination: "[...] perhaps it is not utopian to hope in the action of these two elements —the cultural conception and the justified fear of the repercussions of a future conflagration—to put an end to war, in the near future [...] we can say to ourselves: everything that works for the development of culture also works against war." Psychoanalysis—its theory, its clinical practice— because explicitly integrated into the field of this culture, is also working against death. Affirming a world worked by the reality of Thanatos, it both responds to and unravels a world often thought of as a possible paradise. **Yes, the death drive is there, ineliminable, and culture responds to it.** The two coexist. Our world is *not without reality*.

Freudian References

Freud's texts, now in the public domain, are available in French in a variety of translations. Those of the *Œuvres complètes*, published by the PUF, are not unanimously accepted by psychoanalysts. The translations published by Gallimard and Seuil are to be preferred, but some technical articles are only available from PUF.

INTRODUCTION
Sigmund Freud présenté par lui-même (1925), Paris, Gallimard, coll. "Folio-essais", no 54, 1984.

JONES (Ernest), *The Life and Work of Sigmund Freud* (1953-1957), Volume I: *The Early Years (1856-1900)*, Volume II: *The Years of Maturity (1901-1919)*, Volume III: *The Later Years (1919-1939)*, Paris, PUF, "Quadrige" series, 2006.

THE TRANSFER

Letters to Wilhelm Fließ (1887-1904), complete edition, Paris, PUF, 2006.

FLIESS (Wilhelm), *Les Relations entre le nez et les organes génitaux féminins présentés selon leurs significations biologiques* (1897), Paris, Éditions du Seuil, 1977.

"Remarques sur l'amour de transfert" (1914), in *La Technique psychanalytique*, Paris, PUF, coll. "Quadrige", 2010.

THE UNCONSCIOUS

L'Interprétation du rêve (1900), Paris, Éditions du Seuil, 2010.

La Psychopathologie de la vie quotidienne (1904), Paris, Gallimard, "Folio-essais" collection, no. 530, 1997.

"L'inconscient" (1915), in *Métapsychologie*, Paris, Gallimard, coll. "Folio-essais", no. 30, 1968.

SEXUALITY

Trois essais sur la théorie sexuelle (1905-1924), Paris, Gallimard, "Folio-essais" collection, no. 6, 1987.

"Pulsion et destins des pulsions" (1915), in *Métapsychologie*, Paris, Gallimard, coll. "Folio-essais", no. 30, 1968.

Nouvelles conférences d'introduction à la psychanalyse (1933), XXXIIe Conférence "Angoisse et vie pulsionnelle", Paris, Gallimard, coll. "Folio-essais", no. 126, 1984.

HYSTERIA

In collaboration with BREUER (Joseph), *Études sur l'hystérie* (1895), Paris, PUF, 2010.

"L'étiologie de l'hystérie" (1896), in *Névrose, psychose et perversion*, Paris, PUF, 1973.

"Dora. Fragment d'une analyse d'hystérie" (1905), in *Cinq psychanalyses*, Paris, PUF, coll. "Quadrige", 2008.

OBSESSIONAL NEUROSIS

"Nouvelles remarques sur les psychonévroses de défense" (1896), in *Névrose, psychose et perversion*, Paris, PUF, 1973.

L'Homme aux rats. Journal d'une analyse (1907), Paris, PUF, 1974.

"L'Homme aux rats. Remarques sur un cas de névrose de contrainte" (1909), in *Cinq psychanalyses*, Paris, PUF, coll. "Quadrige", 2008.

PERVERSION

"Quelques conséquences psychiques de la différence anatomique entre les sexes" (1925); "Le fétichisme" (1927), in *La Vie sexuelle*, Paris, PUF, 2009.

"Le clivage du moi dans le processus de défense" (1938), in *Résultats, idées, problèmes. Tome II*, Paris, PUF, 1985.

PSYCHOSIS

SCHREBER (Daniel Paul), *Memoirs of a Neuropath, with supplements and an appendix on the question: "Under what conditions can a person deemed insane be kept in a hospital establishment against his obvious will?"* (1903), Paris, Éditions du Seuil, 1975.

"President Schreber. Remarques psychanalytiques sur un cas de paranoïa *(dementia paranoides)* décrit sous forme autobiographique" (1911), in *Cinq psychanalyses*, Paris, PUF, coll. "Quadrige", 2008.

Lacan (Jacques), *The Seminar. Livre III. Les Psychoses (1955-1956)*, Paris, Éditions du Seuil, 1981.

The war

Le Malaise dans la civilisation (1930), Paris, Éditions du Seuil, "Essais" series, no. 630, 2010.

In collaboration with Einstein (Albert), *Pourquoi la guerre?* (1933), Paris, Rivages Poche, coll. "Petite bibliothèque", no. 488, 2005.

Acknowledgements

*Many thanks to Françoise Santon
for proofreading and correction
manuscripts and proofs*

Table of Contents

9 782315 013708